This book Belongs to

....

Copyright 2021 by **Mini Coloring Studio**

All rights reserved. This book or any portion thethereof
may not be reproduced or used in any manner whatsoever
without the express written permission of the publisher
except for the use of brief quotations in a book review

First printing 2021
ISBN 9798702014777

Would You Rather?
Valentine's Day Edition

How do you play?

At least two players are needed to play this game. Face your opponent and decide who is **Valentine Bear 1** and **Valentine Bear 2**. If you have 3 or 4 players, you can decide which players belong to **Valentine Bear 1** and **Valentine Bear 2**. The goal of the game is to score points by making the other players laugh. The first player to a score of 10 points is the **Round Champion**.

What are the rules?

Valentine Bear 1 starts first. Read the question aloud and choose an answer. The same player will then explain why they chose the answer in the silliest and wackiest way possible. If the reason makes **Valentine Bear 2** laught, then **Valentine Bear 1** scores a funny point. Take turns going back and forth and write down the score.

How do you get started?

Flip a coin. The Valentine Bear that guesses it correctly starts first.

Would you rather

be rich and ugly
or
poor and good-looking?

hold my hand
or
put your arm around
my waidt?

Would you rather

**dress up for a night
on the town
or
stay home in sweats?**

**eat the foot prepared by
your mom
or
your boyfriend?**

Would you rather

kiss in public
or
kiss in private?

let your spouse date your
best friend
or
your arch enemy?

Would you rather

go watch a movie
or
go watch the sunset?

be snowed in with
your crush
or
lay on the beach with
your crush?

Would you rather

hit on someone much
older than you
or
have someone much
older hit on you?

find true love
or
be rich?

Would you rather

have really weird dreams
every single night
or
never have dreams again?

wrestle in a pool of jello
or
chocolate pudding?

Would you rather

have a partner who's shy
or
one who makes you feel shy?

be with a jealous
hardworking girlfriend
or
a lazy but trusting
girlfriend?

Would you rather

go jogging together
or
go to the gym together?

your boyfriend keep
short hair
or
long hair?

Would you rather

jog in the daytime together
or
take strolls at night?

send your partner a
good morning
or
a good night text?

Would you rather

date someone with
no emotions
or
date a complusive liar?

be with someone
who's feared
or
someone who's
loved by all?

Would you rather

have a lover who's
obsessed with pets
or
one who doesn't like pets?

try on your partner's clothes
or
have your partner try
on your clothes?

Would you rather

stay friends with your ex

or

never talk to them again?

experience unrequited love

or

never know how it feels
to be in love?

Would you rather

ask for help
or
figure it out yourseflf?

be able to detect any
lie you hear
or
get away with any
lie you tell?

Would you rather

get with your boss to
get promoted
or
give up the promotion?

be a hopeless romantic
or
hopeful unromantic?

Would you rather

have too many friends
or
too few?

have no taste buds
or
be color blind?

Would you rather

never hear music again
or
lose the ability to read?

create history
or
delete it?

Would you rather

be the richest person
in the world
or
the smartest?

sound like *Jar-Jar binks*
for the rest of your life
or
siri?

Would you rather

talk like Yoda
or
breathe like
Darth Vadler?

age from the neck up
or
the neck down only?

Would you rather

have $1,000,000 now
or
$5,000 a week for the rest
of your life?

become a creative person
or
techniecal person?

Would you rather

become famous
or
powerful?

see the world but live
in poverty
or
stay in one place
and live rich?

Would you rather

be able to speak whale
or
read babies' minds

wake up in the monrning
looking like a giraffe
or
kangaroo?

Would you rather

run naked through
the streets
or
have a naked photo be shared
with everyone you know

have legs as long as
your fingers
or
have fingers as long as
your legs?

Would you rather

go back in time
or
travel to the unknown
future?

forget what you are
saying while in charge
of a huge presentation
or
trip and fly across
the floor in office lobby in
front of all your peers?

Would you rather

give up coffee
or
tea give up 2 hours
of sleep a day?

eat stale cereal
or
stale chips?

Would you rather

dress up like a superhero
or
a carton character?

meet Elton John
or
Taylor Swift?

Would you rather

have one wish today
or
three wishes in 20 years?

eat very spicy
or
very bland food only
for 2 months?

Would you rather

save a partner who's shy
or
one who makes you
feel shy?

let your spouse date your
best friend
or
your arch enemy?

Would you rather

have a foot long nose
or
a foot long tongue?

play on Minecraft
or
play fifa?

Would you rather

live in space
or
under the sea?

have a sumo wrestler
on top of you
or
yourself on top of him?

Would you rather

fight 100 duck-sized horses
or
1 horse-sized duck?

eat an entire stick of butter
or
send an embarrassing email
to your entire company?

Would you rather

have a lifelong free subscription of itunes
or
App Store?

infinite battery life for your cell phone
or
infinite fuel for your car?

Would you rather

be stung by a jellyfish
or
give up facebook for
a week?

lose all your contacts
or
lose $100?

Would you rather

watch tv all the time
or
not watch tv at all?

listen to One Direction
or
Justin Beiber?

Would you rather

give a bad gift to
your boyfriend
or
no gift at all?

make a gift made by hand
or
purchase it from a store?

Would you rather

marry a total stranger
or
have forced intimacy
with one?

have large breasts and
a disfigured body
or
have smaller breasts
with a fantastic body?

Would you rather

not put makeup again
or
not look at yourself again?

take one vocation that
lasts four weeks
or
four vocations that
last one week?

Would you rather

have no friends
or
no internet?

be the subject matter
of gossip
or
never being talked
about at all?

Would you rather

live out of a car
or
live on a boat?

eat a raw onion
or
two raw heads of garlic?

Would you rather

give up meat
or
give up fruit?

have the only beverage you
can drink be water
or
the only food you
can eat be salad?

Would you rather

know how you're
going to die
or
when you're going to die?

be able to have
prevented wwll
or
have prevented influenza?

Would you rather

be caught cheating
or
catch your spouse cheating?

talk with me about
someone you fancy
or
fantasize about it secretly
in your mind?

Would you rather

have one partner
or
multiple partners?

confess your crimes in front
of your children
or
commit the crime in front
of your children?

Would you rather

be a superhero
or
a magic wizard?

be the author of a
best-selling a book
or
star in a movie?

Would you rather

be really cold
or
be really hot?

be able to
breathe underwater
or
be able to run on
top of water?

Would you rather

go on a holiday alone
or
with people you dislike?

be able to smell only
bad-smelling things
or
never be able to
smell again?

Would you rather

gulp a whole bottle of beer
or
milk?

watch a horror movie
on your own
or
a bad comedy with people
you don't like?

Would you rather

be alone
or
be with someone you are moderately happy with it?

eat with your hands
or
use a fork to finish a soup?

Would you rather

play truth or dare,
or
monopoly?

spend a year on a remote
island on your own
or
in a polluted world
with other people?

Would you rather

drive a flying car
or
ride on a robot?

wear your wedding dress
for one whole month
or
a bikini?

Would you rather

be attacked by butterflies
or
flies?

be a boss that is disliked
by everyone
or
the top employee liked
by everyone?

Would you rather

be rich and alone
or
not so rich and surrounded
by lovely friends?

spend a year in a treehouse
or
in a haunted house?

Would you rather

live without Google
or
social media?

spend the evening relaxing
at home alone
or
have a drunken night?

Would you rather

have another lockdown
or
back to normal life with
more virus spreading?

witness the start of
the world
or
the end of it?

Would you rather

be able to pause time
or
be able to read
people's minds?

win the lottery
or
let someone you love win it?

Would you rather

change your name
or
your family?

eat a burger for 1 full year
or
no burger at all?

Would you rather

have no one at your funeral
or
your wedding?

spend a year being homeless
or
in prison?

Would you rather

disappoint your family
or
your friends?

sacrifice your life for
someone you love
or
save someone else life?

Would you rather

be in love with your
best friend
or
have your best friend
be in love with you?

be in quarantine with
your favorite pet
or
with a friend?

Would you rather

be overdressed
or
underdressed?

spend your weekends
with family
or
be making money online?

Would you rather

be known for your kindness
or
intelligence?

be able to fly
or
be invisible?

Would you rather

receive cash
or
physical gifts?

lose your sight
or
memories?

Would you rather

hug a panda
or
a koala?

have a date with a
famous celebrity
or
a famous politician?

Would you rather

find true love
or
a million dollar?

live in a house with your ex
or
with a dog you are afraid
of constantly?

Would you rather

go to jail for 5 years
or
not talk to your love
for 5 years?

save first mother, father
or
10 million dollars?

Would you rather

be deaf
or
dumb?

never eat a pizza again
or
let two puppies die?

Would you rather

have a magic carpet
that flies
or
your own robot?

have a chance to create
a new board game
or
direct a movie?

Would you rather

be a year older
or
5 years younger?

have one eye in the
middle of your head
or
two mouths?

Would you rather

have magical powers
or
be natural?

be able to control
living beings
or
be able to raise the dead?

Would you rather

only be able to talk calmly
or
have a very loud voice?

speak all languages
in the world
or
play all instruments?

Would you rather

have lunch on the
Eiffel tower
or
dinner by the seaside?

fly a helicopter
or
a personal plane?

Would you rather

walk barefoot in a
public toilet
or
get poisoned?

live for 100 years
or
be taken back 10 years?

Would you rather

always be dressed up
or
always be in your pyjamas.

have a very long nose
or
blue eyes?

Would you rather

have tiny hands
or
big feet?

have lived in the 80s
or
90s?

Would you rather

be friends with spider man
or
snowhite?

live in the desert
or
on a deserted island?

Would you rather

be tall and slim
or
short and fat?

have a life rewind button
or
a forward button?

Would you rather

be an adult all your life
or
remain a kid?

look like a fish
or
smell like one?

Would you rather

have a kid with no money
or
no kid and be a millionaire?

be a dancer
or
a singer?

Would you rather

spend the night at a
5-star resort
or
spend it in a tent?

sail around the world
or
climb mount, Everest?

Would you rather

visit every country in
the world
or
live in space?

be in the city
or
stay in the country?

Would you rather

be adventurous
or
relax?

play by the beach
or
try climbing mountains?

Would you rather

go to seeing
or
go shopping?

visit tourist spots
or
discover hidden gems?

Would you rather

go on a party trip
or
a romantic trip?

go on a cruise with friend
or
go camping with crush?

Would you rather

have a Mexican takeout
or
Chinese eat in?

give up music
or
give up tv?

Would you rather

read a book
or
lists to the podcast?

meditate
or
do some journaling?

Would you rather

travel for the rest
of your life
or
stay home forever?

have popcorn
or
chocolate?

Would you rather

take a bubble bath
or
go for a swim?

cook your favourite meal
or
go to your favourite
restaurant?

Would you rather

be single
or
taken?

visit the beach with
your partner
or
stay in all day?

Would you rather

shave all your hard
or
lose a tooth?

have a camera as
your eyes
or
have sound decoder as
your ears?

Would you rather

eat a can of cat food
or
eat three whole lemons?

wear the same clothes to
school every day
or
have your parents pick
your clothes every day?

Would you rather

sit for the rest of your life
or
stand?

run across a hungry
alligator back
or
run underneath an
angry elephant?

Would you rather

be known for being smart
or
for being brave?

be the best player on a
team that always loses
or
be the worst player
that wins?

Would you rather

take a cold shower
or
sleep an hour less
than you need?

lose an arm
or
a leg?

Would you rather

have it all
or
know it all?

have green teeth
or
green hair?

Would you rather

have a friend who is
really fun
or
really nice?

be trapped in a room with
10 screaming babies
or
one hungry alligator?

Would you rather

clean the floor with
your fingernail
or
your toothbrush?

lick the floor
or
lick mouldy trash?

Would you rather

ride a bike on ice
or
roller skate down a
ramp with sand?

bathe in ice cubes
or
battle in tomato soup?

Would you rather

have no teeth
or
no hair?

see a firework display
or
go to Disneyland?

Would you rather

have an extra finger
or
an extra toe?

create a holiday
or
a new language?

Would you rather

eat doughnuts
or
candy?

live on the moon
or
live in Mars?

Would you rather

have 2 sisters
or
2 brothers?

kiss a frog
or
hug a snake?

What do you think about our product?

Don't wait and share your opinion today!